THE *Skinny* NUTRI NINJA RECIPE BOOK

CookNation

THE SKINNY NUTRI NINJA RECIPE BOOK
DELICIOUS & NUTRITIOUS HEALTHY SMOOTHIES UNDER 100, 200 & 300 CALORIES.

ISBN 978-1-910771-76-1

A CIP catalogue record of this book is available from the British Library

DISCLAIMER

This book is designed to provide information on smoothies and juices that can be made in the NUTRiBULLET appliance only, results may differ if alternative devices are used.

Nutri Ninja™ is a registered trademark of SharkNinja Operating LLC. Bell & Mackenzie Publishing is not affiliated with the owner of the trademark and is not an authorized distributor of the trademark owner's products or services. This publication has not been prepared, approved, or licensed by Nutri Ninja ™ or SharkNinja Operating LLC.

Some recipes may contain nuts or traces of nuts. Those suffering from any allergies associated with nuts should avoid any recipes containing nuts or nut based oils.
This information is provided and sold with the knowledge that the publisher and author do not offer any legal or other professional advice.
In the case of a need for any such expertise consult with the appropriate professional.
This book does not contain all information available on the subject, and other sources of recipes are available.
This book has not been created to be specific to any individual's or NUTRiBULLET's requirements.
Every effort has been made to make this book as accurate as possible. However, there may be typographical and or content errors. Therefore, this book should serve only as a general guide and not as the ultimate source of subject information.
This book contains information that might be dated and is intended only to educate and entertain.

The author and publisher shall have no liability or responsibility to any person or entity regarding any loss or damage incurred, or alleged to have incurred, directly or indirectly, by the information contained in this book.

CONTENTS

INTRODUCTION

Just one smoothie a day can make a difference to the way you feel and it only takes seconds to make!

THERE HAS NEVER BEEN A BETTER TIME to introduce health-boosting, weight reducing and well-being smoothies to your life. With a spiralling obesity epidemic in the western world which in turn is linked to a growing list of debilitating diseases and ailments including diabetes, high blood pressure, heart disease, high cholesterol, infertility, skin conditions and more, the future for many of us can look bleak. Combine this with the super-fast pace of modern life and we can be left feeling fatigued and lethargic, worsened by daily consumption of unhealthy foods.

Using the power from a nutrient packed smoothie made in your Ninja is an incredibly fast and efficient way of giving our bodies the goodness they need. Making the most of anti-oxidants to protect your cells, omega 3 fatty acids to help your joints, fibre to aid digestion and protein to build and repair muscles.

Just one smoothie a day can make a difference to the way you feel and it only takes seconds to make!

SUPER JUICE FOR WEIGHT LOSS

Drinking Ninja Super Juices for weight loss can be a great way to aid a diet or weight management program. Our delicious recipes are packed with healthy ingredients, which will help you achieve your recommended daily quota of fruit and veg, yet are light on calories. Replacing just one meal a day with one of our weight loss smoothies will leave you feeling satisfied, knowing that the goodness in a glass is packed with nutrient dense ingredients. By stripping your diet of unhealthy processed foods weight loss becomes effortless and within days you'll feel brighter, stronger, more energetic and focussed.

Benefits can include:

WEIGHT LOSS · REJUVENATION · GLOWING SKIN · INCREASED ENERGY · LOWER BLOOD PRESSURE · LOWER CHOLESTEROL

and overall enhanced wellbeing.

The Skinny Nutri Ninja Recipe book is packed with over 80 delicious and simple recipes.

All our recipes make use of the 24 oz cup of the Nutri Ninja and the extractor blade. We encourage you to experiment with your smoothies, mixing your ingredients is fun and will help your create wonderful new super juices.
As a basic formula work on 50% leafy greens 50% fruit, ¼ cup of seeds/nuts and water.
We hope you enjoy our recipes.

TIPS

To help make your smoothies fuss-free, follow these quick tips.

- Prepare your shopping list. Take some time to select which drinks you want to prepare in advance. As with all food shopping, make a note of all the ingredients and quantities you need. Depending on the ingredients it's best not to shop too far in advance to ensure you are getting the freshest produce available. We recommend buying organic produce whenever you can if your budget allows. Organic produce can give a better yield and flavour to your smoothie. Remember almost all fruit is fine to freeze too.
- Wash your fruit and veg before juicing. This needn't take up much time but all produce should be washed clean of any traces of bacteria, pesticides and insects.
- To save time prepare produce the night before for early morning smoothies.
- Cut up any produce that may not fit into the cup, but only do this just before juicing to keep it as fresh as possible.
- Wash your Nutri Ninja parts immediately after juicing. As tempting as it may be to leave it till a little later you'll be glad you took the few minutes to rinse and wash before any residue has hardened.
- Substitute where you need to. If you can't source a particular ingredient, try another instead. More often than not you will find the use of a different fruit or veg makes a really interesting and delicious alternative. In our recipes we offer some advice on alternatives but have the confidence to make your own too!
- Some smoothies are sweeter than others and it's a fact that some of the leafy green drinks can take a little getting used to. Try drinking these with a straw, you'll find them easier to drink and enjoy.
- Drink lots of water!

IMPORTANT – WHAT NOT TO USE IN YOUR NUTRI NINJA

While the joy of making smoothies is using whole fruit and vegetables there are a few seeds and pits which should be removed. The following contain chemicals which can release cyanide into the body when ingested so do not use any of the following in your smoothies:

- **Apple Seeds**
- **Cherry Pits**
- **Peach pits**
- **Apricot Pits**
- **Plum Pits**

CLEANING

Cleaning the Nutri Ninja is thankfully very easy. The manufacturer gives clear guidelines on how best to do this but here's a recap:

Make sure the Nuti Ninja is unplugged before disassembling or cleaning.
Set aside the power base and blade holders as these should not be used in a dishwasher.
Use hot soapy water to clean the blades but do not immerse in boiling water as this can warp the plastic.

Use a damp cloth to clean the power base.
All cups and lids can be placed in a dishwasher.
For stubborn marks inside the cup, fill the cup to the max line with warm soapy water and attach the blade assembly then pulse for a few times.

WARNING:

Do not put your hands or any utensils near the moving blade. Always ensure the Nuti Ninjanis unplugged when assembling/disassembling or cleaning.

Do not process dry ingredients without adding liquid to the cup.

ABOUT COOKNATION

CookNation is the leading publisher of innovative and practical recipe books for the modern, health conscious cook.

CookNation titles bring together delicious, easy and practical recipes with their unique approach - easy and delicious, no-nonsense recipes - making cooking for diets and healthy eating fast, simple and fun.

With a range of #1 best-selling titles - from the innovative 'Skinny' calorie-counted series, to the 5:2 Diet Recipes collection - CookNation recipe books prove that 'Diet' can still mean 'Delicious'!

Turn to the end of this book to browse all CookNation's recipe books

Skinny NUTRI NINJA

UNDER 100 CALORIES

SERVES 1

APRICOT & SPINACH BLAST

98 calories

Ingredients

LEAFY GREENS

- 40g/1½oz spinach
- 40g/1½oz Swiss chard
- 175g/6oz fresh apricots
- Water

Method

1 Rinse the ingredients well.

2 Cut any thick green stalks off the spinach.

3 Halve and stone the apricots.

4 Add the fruit & vegetables to the . Make sure the ingredients do not go past the MAX line on your machine.

5 Add water, again being careful not to exceed the MAX line.

6 Twist on the Ninja blade and blend until smooth.

CHEF'S NOTE

It's fine to use extra spinach in place of the Swiss chard.

SERVES 1

DOUBLE BERRY BLAST

95
calories

Ingredients

BLUEBERRY POWER

- 40g/1½oz spinach
- 75g/3oz blueberries
- 75g/3oz blackberries
- Water

Method

1 Rinse the ingredients well.

2 Cut any thick green stalks off the spinach.

3 Add the fruit & vegetables to the . Make sure the ingredients do not go past the MAX line on your machine.

4 Add water, again being careful not to exceed the MAX line.

5 Twist on the Ninja blade and blend until smooth.

CHEF'S NOTE

Any mix of soft berries will work for this simple smoothie. If it's a little sharp add 1 tsp honey (21 calories).

SUNNY PEACH GREENS

SERVES 1

85 calories

Ingredients

GOOD & GREEN

- 40g/1½oz spinach
- 40g/1½oz broccoli
- 125g/4oz stoned peach halves
- Water

Method

1. Rinse the ingredients well.
2. Cut any thick green stalks off the spinach.
3. Add the fruit & vegetables to the Ninja large (24oz) cup. Make sure the ingredients do not go past the MAX line on your machine.
4. Add water, again being careful not to exceed the MAX line.
5. Twist on the Ninja blade and blend until smooth.

CHEF'S NOTE

Broccoli's fibre related components help aid digestion.

SERVES 1

BLUEBERRY BROCCOLINI

99 calories

Ingredients

SKIN CLEANSER

- 75g/3oz tenderstem broccoli/broccolini
- 75g/3oz blueberries
- 1 tsp honey
- Water

Method

1 Rinse the ingredients well.

2 Cut any thick woody ends off the broccoli.

3 Add the fruit, vegetables and honey to the . Make sure the ingredients do not go past the MAX line on your machine.

4 Add water, again being careful not to exceed the MAX line.

5 Twist on the Ninja blade and blend until smooth.

CHEF'S NOTE

Purple sprouting broccoli is a lovely tenderstem broccoli to use when it's in season.

SERVES 1

BERRY ALMOND MILK SMOOTHIE

98 calories

Ingredients

FRUITY & SWEET!

- 40g/1½oz blackberries
- 40g/1½oz raspberries
- 100ml/3½floz unsweetened almond milk
- Water

Method

1 Rinse the ingredients well.

2 Add the fruit & almond milk to the Ninja large (24oz) cup. Make sure the ingredients do not go past the MAX line on your machine.

3 Add water, again being careful not to exceed the MAX line.

4 Twist on the Ninja blade and blend until smooth.

CHEF'S NOTE

Adjust the quantity of water to get the consistency you prefer.

SERVES 1

RASPBERRY PAPAYA SMOOTHIE

96 calories

Ingredients

NUTRIENT RICH

- 75g/3oz raspberries
- 75g/3oz papaya
- 50g/2oz carrots
- Water

Method

1. Rinse the ingredients well.
2. Top & tail the carrots.
3. Add the berries, carrots & papaya to the Ninja large (24oz) cup. Make sure the ingredients do not go past the MAX line on your machine.
4. Add water, again being careful not to exceed the MAX line.
5. Twist on the Ninja blade and blend until smooth.

CHEF'S NOTE

Don't bother peeling the carrot, just nip the root top off.

SERVES 1

COCONUT GREEN SMOOTHIE

95 calories

Ingredients

LIGHT & FRESH!

- 75g/3oz spinach
- 400ml/14floz coconut water
- Handful of ice cubes (optional)

Method

1 Rinse the spinach and remove any thick stalks.

2 Add the spinach & coconut water to the Ninja large (24oz) cup. Make sure the ingredients do not go past the MAX line on your machine. (If you are adding ice cubes you may need to use a little less coconut water).

3 Twist on the Ninja blade and blend until smooth.

CHEF'S NOTE

It's best to use unsweetened 100% coconut water.

SERVES 1

SWEET STRAWBERRY COCONUT WATER

98 calories

Ingredients

REFRESHING!

- 75g/3oz strawberries
- 300ml/10½floz coconut water
- 1 tsp honey
- Water

Method

1 Rinse well and remove the green tops from the strawberries.

2 Add the honey, strawberries & coconut water to the Ninja large (24oz) cup. Make sure the ingredients do not go past the MAX line on your machine.

3 Add a little water if needed to take it up to the MAX line.

4 Twist on the Ninja blade and blend until smooth.

CHEF'S NOTE

This is a really light refreshing juice. Serve with lots of crushed ice.

SERVES 1

FRESH TOMATO & ALMOND MILK SMOOTHIE

96 calories

Ingredients

LYCOPENE +

- 150g/5oz ripe tomatoes
- 100ml/3½floz unsweetened almond milk
- Water

Method

1 Rinse the tomatoes, remove any green stalks from the tops and cut in half.

2 Add the tomatoes & almond milk to the Ninja large (24oz) cup. Make sure the ingredients do not go past the MAX line on your machine.

3 Add water (you may wish to add only a little if you want a thicker consistency), again being careful not to exceed the MAX line.

4 Twist on the Ninja blade and blend until smooth.

CHEF'S NOTE

Use really ripe vine-ripened tomatoes to get the benefit of their natural sweetness.

SERVES 1

CARROT & RASPBERRY JUICE

100 calories

Ingredients

MULTI VITAMINS

- 75g/3oz raspberries
- 150g/5oz carrots
- Water

Method

1 Rinse the ingredients well.

2 Top & tail the carrots, no need to peel.

3 Add the raspberries & carrots to the Ninja large (24oz) cup. Make sure the ingredients do not go past the MAX line on your machine.

4 Add water, again being careful not to exceed the MAX line.

5 Twist on the Ninja blade and blend until smooth.

CHEF'S NOTE

Add a dash of Tabasco/hot sauce to this simple juice is you wish and serve with a stick of fresh celery.

GREEN CAULIFLOWER SMOOTHIE

SERVES 1

97 calories

Ingredients

CREAMY!

- 75g/3oz cauliflower florets
- 75g/3oz watercress
- 100ml/3½floz unsweetened almond milk
- 1 tsp honey
- Water

Method

1 Rinse the ingredients well.

2 Add the cauliflower, watercress, honey & almond milk to the Ninja large (24oz) cup. Make sure the ingredients do not go past the MAX line on your machine.

3 Add water, again being careful not to exceed the MAX line.

4 Twist on the Ninja blade and blend until smooth.

CHEF'S NOTE

Cauliflower is a surprisingly good source of Vitamin C.

SERVES 1

WATERCRESS & APRICOT JUICE

99
calories

Ingredients

DIETARY NITRATE

- 75g/3oz watercress
- 175g/6oz fresh apricots
- Water

Method

1 Rinse the ingredients well.

2 Halve and stone the apricots.

3 Add the watercress & apricots to the Ninja large (24oz) cup. Make sure the ingredients do not go past the MAX line on your machine.

4 Add water, again being careful not to exceed the MAX line.

5 Twist on the Ninja blade and blend until smooth.

CHEF'S NOTE

Part of the cruciferous/brassica family, watercress is closely related to kale and broccoli.

RUBY MILK

SERVES 1

99
calories

Ingredients

VIBRANT COLOUR!

- 75g/3oz fresh beetroot
- 50g/2oz carrots
- 100ml/3½floz unsweetened almond milk
- Water

Method

1. Rinse the ingredients well.
2. Peel and dice the beetroot. Top, tail and chop the carrot.
3. Add the diced beetroot, carrot & almond milk to the Ninja large (24oz) cup. Make sure the ingredients do not go past the MAX line on your machine.
4. Add water, again being careful not to exceed the MAX line.
5. Twist on the Ninja blade and blend until smooth.

CHEF'S NOTE

The combination of almond milk and water help to keep the calories low.

SERVES 1

GREEN FRUIT CASHEWS

96 calories

Ingredients

MINERAL RICH

- 50g/2oz spinach
- 100g/3½oz strawberries
- 1 tbsp cashew nuts
- Water

Method

1. Rinse the ingredients well.
2. Cut any thick green stalks off the spinach and remove the green tops from the strawberries.
3. Add the fruit & nuts to the Ninja large (24oz) cup. Make sure the ingredients do not go past the MAX line on your machine.
4. Add water, again being careful not to exceed the MAX line.
5. Twist on the Ninja blade and blend until smooth.

CHEF'S NOTE

Cashew nuts contain vitamins E, K, and B6, along with minerals copper, phosphorus, zinc, magnesium, iron, and selenium.

SERVES 1

CHINESE PINEAPPLE JUICE

92 calories

Ingredients

DIETARY FIBRE

- 75g/3oz pak choi/bok choi
- 150g/5oz fresh pineapple
- Water

Method

1 Rinse the ingredients well.

2 Cut any thick woody ends off the pak choi.

3 Add the fruit & vegetables to the Ninja large (24oz) cup. Make sure the ingredients do not go past the MAX line on your machine.

4 Add water, again being careful not to exceed the MAX line.

5 Twist on the Ninja blade and blend until smooth.

CHEF'S NOTE

Any leafy green will work fine in place of Asian inspired pak choi.

SERVES 1

APPLE & CARROT TONIC

90 calories

Ingredients

FLAVANOIDS+

- 75g/3oz spinach
- 50g/2oz carrot
- 100g/3½oz apple
- Water

Method

1 Rinse the ingredients well.

2 Cut any thick green stalks off the spinach.

3 Core the apple. Top & tail the carrot, no need to peel.

4 Add the fruit & vegetables to the Ninja large (24oz) cup. Make sure the ingredients do not go past the MAX line on your machine.

5 Add water, again being careful not to exceed the MAX line.

6 Twist on the Ninja blade and blend until smooth.

CHEF'S NOTE

Carrot and apple are a classic antioxidant juice combo.

SERVES 1

SWEET PEPPER & APPLE JUICE

99 calories

Ingredients

VITAMIN C

- 75g/3oz watercress
- 1 medium red pepper
- 75g/3oz apple
- Water

Method

1. Rinse the ingredients well.
2. De-seed and core the red pepper & apple.
3. Add the fruit & watercress to the Ninja large (24oz) cup. Make sure the ingredients do not go past the MAX line on your machine.
4. Add water, again being careful not to exceed the MAX line.
5. Twist on the Ninja blade and blend until smooth.

CHEF'S NOTE

Add a little fresh chilli to this for a spicy 'kick'.

SERVES 1

BERRY & CELERY COCONUT JUICE

93 calories

Ingredients

NATURALLY ISOTONIC

- 50g/2oz raspberries
- 75g/3oz celery stalks
- 300ml/10½floz coconut water
- Water

Method

1 Rinse the ingredients well.

2 Cut any thick ends off the celery stalks.

3 Add the raspberries, celery & coconut water to the Ninja large (24oz) cup. Make sure the ingredients do not go past the MAX line on your machine.

4 Add a little water if needed to take it up to the MAX line.

5 Twist on the Ninja blade and blend until smooth.

CHEF'S NOTE

You can use blueberries or blackberries in place of raspberries.

SERVES 1

ITALIAN HERB JUICE

60 calories

Ingredients

GOOD FOR SKIN

- 3 tbsp fresh basil leaves
- 75g/3oz spinach
- 2 tsp honey
- Water

Method

1 Rinse the ingredients well.

2 Cut any thick stalks off the spinach.

3 Add the basil, spinach & honey to the Ninja large (24oz) cup. Make sure the ingredients do not go past the MAX line on your machine.

4 Add water, again being careful not to exceed the MAX line.

5 Twist on the Ninja blade and blend until smooth.

CHEF'S NOTE

A little fresh mint is also good added to this simple aromatic juice.

SERVES 1

CELERY CLEANSER

46 calories

Ingredients

ANTIOXIDANTS

- 50g/2oz spinach
- 75g/3oz celery stalks
- 150g/5oz cucumber
- 2 tbsp lemon juice
- Water

Method

1. Rinse the ingredients well.
2. Cut any thick ends off the celery stalks.
3. Add the spinach, celery, cucumber & lemon juice to the Ninja large (24oz) cup. Make sure the ingredients do not go past the MAX line on your machine.
4. Add water, again being careful not to exceed the MAX line.
5. Twist on the Ninja blade and blend until smooth.

CHEF'S NOTE

You could add some chopped apple or carrot to sweeten the juice if you prefer.

SERVES 1

LIGHT GOJI BERRY JUICE

80 calories

Ingredients

ANTI-AGING

- 50g/2oz spinach
- 2 tbsp lime juice
- 3 tbsp goji berries
- Handful of ice
- Water

Method

1. Rinse the ingredients well.
2. Remove any thick stalks from the spinach.
3. Add the spinach, lime juice, goji berries & ice to the Ninja large (24oz) cup. Make sure the ingredients do not go past the MAX line on your machine.
4. Add a little water if needed to take it up to the MAX line.
5. Twist on the Ninja blade and blend until smooth.

CHEF'S NOTE

Fresh and light this simple juice is jam-packed with vitamins.

Skinny NUTRI NINJA

UNDER 200 CALORIES

PEAR PEPPER JUICE

SERVES 1

130 calories

Ingredients

FOLATE SOURCE

- 75g/3oz spinach
- 1 medium yellow pepper
- 75g/3oz ripe pear
- Water

Method

1. Rinse the ingredients well.
2. Remove any thick stalks from the spinach.
3. De-seed and core the yellow pepper & pear.
4. Add the fruit & spinach to the Ninja large (24oz) cup. Make sure the ingredients do not go past the MAX line on your machine.
5. Add water, again being careful not to exceed the MAX line.
6. Twist on the Ninja blade and blend until smooth.

CHEF'S NOTE

Any coloured sweet pepper will work for this juice (not green though as it has a bitter taste).

SERVES 1

FRUITY COCONUT MILK

199
calories

Ingredients

NATURAL SUGAR

- 75g/3oz strawberries
- 200ml/7floz light coconut milk
- ½ small banana
- Water

Method

1 Rinse well and remove the green tops from the strawberries.

2 Peel the banana.

3 Add the strawberries, coconut milk & banana to the Ninja large (24oz) cup. Make sure the ingredients do not go past the MAX line on your machine.

4 Add a little water if needed to take it up to the MAX line.

5 Twist on the Ninja blade and blend until smooth.

CHEF'S NOTE

Make sure you use low fat coconut milk not the full fat version.

SERVES 1

CARROT & KIWI JUICE

173
calories

Ingredients

BETA CAROTENE

- 150g/5oz kiwi
- 200g/7oz carrots
- Water

Method

1. Rinse the ingredients well.
2. Peel the kiwis and slice.
3. Top & tail the carrots, no need to peel.
4. Add the sliced kiwi & carrots to the Ninja large (24oz) cup. Make sure the ingredients do not go past the MAX line on your machine.
5. Add water, again being careful not to exceed the MAX line.
6. Twist on the Ninja blade and blend until smooth.

CHEF'S NOTE

The kiwi fruit is a great source of copper and dietary fibre.

SERVES 1

SWEET CARROT & SPINACH

172 calories

Ingredients

VITAMIN POWERHOUSE

- 50g/2oz spinach
- 150g/5oz apples
- 200g/7oz carrots
- Water

Method

1. Rinse the ingredients well.
2. Cut any thick green stalks off the spinach.
3. Peel and core the apples.
4. Top & tail the carrots, no need to peel.
5. Add the fruit and vegetables to the Ninja large (24oz) cup. Make sure the ingredients do not go past the MAX line on your machine.
6. Add water, again being careful not to exceed the MAX line.
7. Twist on the Ninja blade and blend until smooth.

CHEF'S NOTE

The apple and carrot work together to create a naturally sweet base for this juice.

SERVES 1

CRANBERRY & BROCCOLI MINT JUICE

132 calories

Ingredients

IMMUNE BOOSTER!

- 125g/4oz cranberries
- 75g/3oz broccoli florets
- 1 tbsp chopped mint
- 1 tbsp pumpkin seeds
- Water

Method

1 Rinse the ingredients well.

2 Add the fruit, vegetables, mint & pumpkin seeds to the Ninja large (24oz) cup. Make sure the ingredients do not go past the MAX line on your machine.

3 Add water, again being careful not to exceed the MAX line.

4 Twist on the Ninja blade and blend until smooth.

CHEF'S NOTE

Cranberries are thought to have a positive effect on the immune system.

SERVES 1

NUTTY CABBAGE & PEAR

196 calories

Ingredients

LOWERS CHOLESTEROL

- 75g/3oz shredded white cabbage
- 75g/3oz pears
- 200ml/7floz light coconut milk
- Water

Method

1. Rinse the ingredients well.
2. Core the pear.
3. Add the cabbage, pear & coconut milk to the Ninja large (24oz) cup. Make sure the ingredients do not go past the MAX line on your machine.
4. Add a little water if needed to take it up to the MAX line.
5. Twist on the Ninja blade and blend until smooth.

CHEF'S NOTE

Rich in vitamin C cabbage is also a good source of manganese.

SERVES 1

KALE & CINNAMON JUICE

195 calories

Ingredients

LOWERS BLOOD SUGAR

- 75g/3oz kale
- ½ small banana
- 100g/3½oz apples
- 200ml/7floz coconut water
- 1 tsp ground cinnamon

Method

1 Rinse the ingredients well.

2 Cut any thick green stalks off the kale.

3 Core the apple and peel the banana.

4 Add the vegetables, fruit, coconut water & ground cinnamon to the Ninja large (24oz) cup. Make sure the ingredients do not go past the MAX line on your machine.

5 Add a little water if needed to take it up to the MAX line.

6 Twist on the Ninja blade and blend until smooth.

CHEF'S NOTE

Cinnamon has been used throughout the ages to treat everything from the common cold to muscle spasms.

SERVES 1

BEETROOT SALAD BOOST

160 calories

Ingredients

- 75g/3oz fresh beetroot
- 75g/3oz shredded lettuce leaves
- 150g/5oz apples
- 1 tbsp flax seeds
- Water

Method

1 Rinse the ingredients well.

2 Peel the beetroot.

3 Core the apple.

4 Add the fruit, vegetables & flax seeds to the Ninja large (24oz) cup. Make sure the ingredients do not go past the MAX line on your machine.

5 Add water, again being careful not to exceed the MAX line.

6 Twist on the Ninja blade and blend until smooth.

CHEF'S NOTE

Flax seeds are a high-fibre super food rich in Omega-3 essential fatty acids.

SERVES 1

COURGETTE & MANGO SMOOTHIE

199 calories

Ingredients

POTASSIUM +

- 50g/2oz spinach
- 75g/3oz courgettes/zucchini
- 100g/3½oz mango
- 200ml/7floz unsweetened almond milk
- Water

Method

1 Rinse the ingredients well.

2 Cut any thick green stalks off the spinach. Nip the ends off the courgettes.

3 Peel and stone the mango.

4 Add the fruit, vegetables & almond milk to the Ninja large (24oz) cup. Make sure the ingredients do not go past the MAX line on your machine.

5 Add a little water if needed to take it up to the MAX line.

6 Twist on the Ninja blade and blend until smooth.

CHEF'S NOTE

Almond milk is low in fat, high in energy proteins, lipids and fibre.

SERVES 1

ALMOND CARROT SMOOTHIE

195 calories

Ingredients

- 50g/2oz spinach
- 125g/4oz carrots
- 200ml/7floz unsweetened almond milk
- 1 tbsp ground almonds
- Water

Method

1 Rinse the ingredients well.

2 Cut any thick green stalks off the spinach.

3 Top & tail the carrots, no need to peel.

4 Add the vegetables, almond milk & ground almonds to the Ninja large (24oz) cup. Make sure the ingredients do not go past the MAX line on your machine.

5 Add a little water if needed to take it up to the MAX line.

6 Twist on the Ninja blade and blend until smooth.

CHEF'S NOTE

The ground almonds help create a thick base for this double nut smoothie.

APRICOT & SALAD JUICE

SERVES 1

178 calories

Ingredients

- 50g/2oz shredded lettuce
- 125g/4oz carrots
- 175g/6oz fresh apricots
- 200ml/7floz coconut water
- Water

Method

1. Rinse the ingredients well.
2. Top & tail the carrots, no need to peel.
3. Halve and stone the apricots.
4. Add the fruit, vegetables & coconut water to the Ninja large (24oz) cup. Make sure the ingredients do not go past the MAX line on your machine.
5. Add a little water if needed to take it up to the MAX line.
6. Twist on the Ninja blade and blend until smooth.

CHEF'S NOTE

Coconut water is a good source of B vitamins and potassium.

SERVES 1

SUNSHINE RADISH SMOOTHIE

189 calories

Ingredients

- 50g/2oz spinach
- 200g/7oz pink grapefruit
- 125g/4oz radishes
- 200ml/7floz unsweetened almond milk
- Water

Method

1 Rinse the ingredients well.

2 Cut any thick green stalks off the spinach.

3 Peel and de-seed the grapefruit

4 Nip the tops of the radishes.

5 Add the fruit, vegetables & almond milk to the Ninja large (24oz) cup. Make sure the ingredients do not go past the MAX line on your machine.

6 Add a little water if needed to take it up to the MAX line.

7 Twist on the Ninja blade and blend until smooth.

CHEF'S NOTE

Any type of grapefruit is fine to use but pink will give you the best result.

MELON & WATERCRESS SMOOTHIE

SERVES 1

199 calories

Ingredients

VITAMIN A+

- 50g/2oz watercress
- 200g/7oz melon flesh
- 50g/2oz fresh tomatoes
- 200ml/7floz light coconut milk
- Water

Method

1 Rinse the ingredients well.

2 Add the fruit, vegetables & coconut milk to the Ninja large (24oz) cup. Make sure the ingredients do not go past the MAX line on your machine.

3 Add a little water if needed to take it up to the MAX line.

4 Twist on the Ninja blade and blend until smooth.

CHEF'S NOTE

Use sweet melon flesh such as honeydew rather than watermelon for this smoothie.

SERVES 1

PEACH & SPINACH ALMOND SMOOTHIE

197 calories

HEALTHY SKIN

- 50g/2oz spinach
- 150g/5oz peach
- 200ml/7floz unsweetened almond milk
- Water

Method

1. Rinse the ingredients well.
2. Cut any thick green stalks off the spinach
3. Peel and stone the peach.
4. Add the spinach, peach & almond milk to the Ninja large (24oz) cup. Make sure the ingredients do not go past the MAX line on your machine.
5. Add a little water if needed to take it up to the MAX line.
6. Twist on the Ninja blade and blend until smooth.

CHEF'S NOTE

This is also good with soya milk in place of almond milk.

SERVES 1

CARROT & COCONUT WATER JUICE

138 calories

Ingredients

BONE STRENGTHENING

- 50g/2oz spinach
- 200g/7oz carrots
- 200ml/7floz coconut water
- Water

Method

1. Rinse the ingredients well.
2. Cut any thick green stalks off the spinach
3. Top & tail the carrots, no need to peel.
4. Add the vegetables & coconut water to the Ninja large (24oz) cup. Make sure the ingredients do not go past the MAX line on your machine.
5. Add a little water if needed to take it up to the MAX line.
6. Twist on the Ninja blade and blend until smooth.

CHEF'S NOTE

For a thicker blend substitute the water for light coconut milk.

LEMON DETOX JUICE

SERVES 1

186 calories

Ingredients

- 50g/2oz spinach
- 200g/7oz apples
- 3 tbsp lemon juice
- 1 tbsp chia seeds
- Water

Method

1 Rinse the ingredients well.

2 Cut any thick green stalks off the spinach

3 Core the apple.

4 Add the spinach, apple, chia seeds & lemon juice to the Ninja large (24oz) cup. Make sure the ingredients do not go past the MAX line on your machine.

5 Add water, again being careful not to exceed the MAX line.

6 Twist on the Ninja blade and blend until smooth.

CHEF'S NOTE

Adjust the lemon juice to suit your own taste.

SERVES 1

SUPER GREEN CUCUMBER JUICE

186 calories

Ingredients

HYDRATING

- 50g/2oz spinach
- 150g/5oz cucumber
- 2 tbsp lemon juice
- 1 tbsp flax seed
- Water

Method

1. Rinse the ingredients well.
2. Cut any thick green stalks off the spinach.
3. Nip the end of the cucumber but don't bother peeling it.
4. Add the spinach, cucumber, lemon juice & flax seed to the Ninja large (24oz) cup. Make sure the ingredients do not go past the MAX line on your machine.
5. Add water, again being careful not to exceed the MAX line.
6. Twist on the Ninja blade and blend until smooth.

CHEF'S NOTE

Cucumbers contain vitamin K, B vitamins, copper, potassium, vitamin C, and manganese.

SERVES 1

GINGER & BLACKBERRY SMOOTHIE

160 calories

Ingredients

- 50g/2oz watercress
- 150g/5oz blackberries
- 1 small banana
- 2cm/1 inch peeled fresh ginger root
- Water

Method

1 Rinse the ingredients well.

2 Peel the banana.

3 Add the watercress, blackberries, banana & ginger to the Ninja large (24oz) cup. Make sure the ingredients do not go past the MAX line on your machine.

4 Add water, again being careful not to exceed the MAX line.

5 Twist on the Ninja blade and blend until smooth.

CHEF'S NOTE

Ginger contains gingerol, which has powerful medicinal properties.

SERVES 1 SPICY PUMPKIN SEED TOMATO JUICE

110 calories

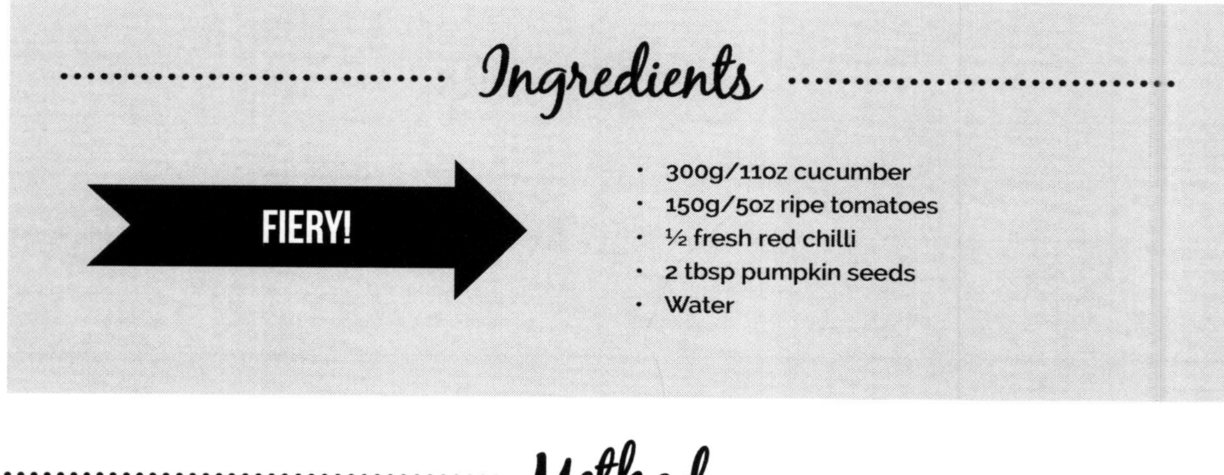

Ingredients

- 300g/11oz cucumber
- 150g/5oz ripe tomatoes
- ½ fresh red chilli
- 2 tbsp pumpkin seeds
- Water

Method

1 Rinse the ingredients well.

2 Nip the ends off the cucumber but don't bother peeling.

3 De-seed the chilli.

4 Add the cucumber, tomatoes, chilli & pumpkin seeds to the Ninja large (24oz) cup. Make sure the ingredients do not go past the MAX line on your machine.

5 Add water, again being careful not to exceed the MAX line.

6 Twist on the Ninja blade and blend until smooth.

CHEF'S NOTE

Adjust the chilli quantity to suit your own taste.

SERVES 1

RASPBERRY & CINNAMON SMOOTHIE

190 calories

Ingredients

- 50g/2oz spinach
- 150g/5oz raspberries
- 200ml/7floz unsweetened almond milk
- 1 tsp ground cinnamon
- Water

Method

1 Rinse the ingredients well.

2 Cut any thick green stalks off the spinach

3 Add the spinach, raspberries, almond milk & ground cinnamon to the Ninja large (24oz) cup. Make sure the ingredients do not go past the MAX line on your machine.

4 Add a little water if needed to take it up to the MAX line.

5 Twist on the Ninja blade and blend until smooth.

CHEF'S NOTE

Try soya milk in place of almond milk as an alternative.

TRIPLE FRUIT BANANA SMOOTHIE

SERVES 1

195 calories

Ingredients

NATURALLY SWEET

- 100g/3½oz apples
- 100g/3½oz pears
- 1 small banana
- Water

Method

1 Rinse the ingredients well.

2 Core the apple & pear. Peel the banana.

3 Add all the fruit to the Ninja large (24oz) cup. Make sure the ingredients do not go past the MAX line on your machine.

4 Add water, again being careful not to exceed the MAX line.

5 Twist on the Ninja blade and blend until smooth.

CHEF'S NOTE

Sweet and simple this is a great 'beginners' smoothie.

SUPER GREEN JUICE

SERVES 1

193 calories

Ingredients

- 50g/2oz spinach
- 50g/2oz kale
- 200g/7oz cucumber
- 175g/6oz apple
- 1 tbsp flax seeds
- Water

Method

1. Rinse the ingredients well.
2. Cut any thick green stalks off the spinach and kale.
3. Core the apple. Nip the ends off the cucumber but don't bother peeling.
4. Add the green leaves, cucumber, apple & flax seeds to the Ninja large (24oz) cup. Make sure the ingredients do not go past the MAX line on your machine.
5. Add water, again being careful not to exceed the MAX line.
6. Twist on the Ninja blade and blend until smooth.

CHEF'S NOTE

Some green smoothies can take a bit of getting used to. Try sipping through a straw until you become accustomed to the taste.

SERVES 1

CASHEW GREENS

195 calories

Ingredients

MAGNESIUM SOURCE

- 50g/2oz spinach
- 200g/7oz melon flesh
- 125g/4oz apple
- 1 tbsp cashew nuts
- Water

Method

1 Rinse the ingredients well.

2 Cut any thick green stalks off the spinach.

3 Core the apple.

4 Add the spinach, melon, apple & cashew nuts to the Ninja large (24oz) cup. Make sure the ingredients do not go past the MAX line on your machine.

5 Add water, again being careful not to exceed the MAX line.

6 Twist on the Ninja blade and blend until smooth.

CHEF'S NOTE

Cashew nuts give a lovely smooth texture to this juice, you could also use almond milk instead of water for the base.

PEPPERY ROCKET JUICE

SERVES 1

142 calories

Ingredients

- 50g/2oz spinach
- 50g/2oz rocket
- 200g/7oz carrots
- 1 tbsp flax seed
- Water

Method

1 Rinse the ingredients well.

2 Cut any thick green stalks off the spinach.

3 Top & tail the carrots, no need to peel.

4 Add the spinach, rocket, carrot & flax seed to the Ninja large (24oz) cup. Make sure the ingredients do not go past the MAX line on your machine.

5 Add water, again being careful not to exceed the MAX line.

6 Twist on the Ninja blade and blend until smooth.

CHEF'S NOTE

You could also add a pinch of cayenne pepper or paprika to complement the natural peppery taste of the rocket.

SERVES 1

TOMATO NINJABLAST

120 calories

Ingredients

OMEGA 3+

- 150g/5oz ripe tomatoes
- 75g/3oz carrots
- 1 tbsp chia seeds
- Water

Method

1 Rinse the ingredients well.

2 Top & tail the carrots, no need to peel.

3 Add the tomatoes, carrots & chia seeds to the Ninja large (24oz) cup. Make sure the ingredients do not go past the MAX line on your machine.

4 Add water, again being careful not to exceed the MAX line.

5 Twist on the Ninja blade and blend until smooth.

CHEF'S NOTE

Chia seeds are a very popular super-food prized for their high protein and essential fatty acid content.

SERVES 1

BANANA, CHIA & SPINACH SMOOTHIE

170 calories

Ingredients

- 50g/2oz spinach
- ½ small banana
- 100ml/3½floz unsweetened almond milk
- 1 tbsp chia seeds
- Water

Method

1 Rinse the ingredients well.

2 Cut any thick green stalks off the spinach.

3 Peel the banana.

4 Add the spinach, banana, milk & chia seeds to the Ninja large (24oz) cup. Make sure the ingredients do not go past the MAX line on your machine.

5 Add a little water if needed to take it up to the MAX line.

6 Twist on the Ninja blade and blend until smooth.

CHEF'S NOTE

Great for breakfast, the high protein chia seeds will help you feel fuller for longer.

SERVES 1

MINTED CITRUS JUICE

148 calories

Ingredients

SOOTHING MINT

- 200g/7oz oranges
- 100g/3½oz apple
- 1 tbsp fresh mint
- Water

Method

1. Rinse the ingredients well.
2. Peel and de-seed the oranges.
3. Core the apple.
4. Add the fruit & mint to the Ninja large (24oz) cup. Make sure the ingredients do not go past the MAX line on your machine.
5. Add water, again being careful not to exceed the MAX line.
6. Twist on the Ninja blade and blend until smooth.

CHEF'S NOTE

Mint is a potent herb that helps aid digestion.

Skinny NUTRI NINJA

UNDER 300 CALORIES

SERVES 1

STRAWBERRY DOUBLE NUT SMOOTHIE

262 calories

Ingredients

- 150g/5oz strawberries
- 1 small banana
- 200ml/7floz unsweetened almond milk
- 1 tbsp ground almonds
- Water

Method

1. Rinse the ingredients well.
2. Remove any green tops from the strawberries.
3. Peel the banana.
4. Add the fruit, milk & ground almonds to the Ninja large (24oz) cup. Make sure the ingredients do not go past the MAX line on your machine.
5. Add a little water if needed to take it up to the MAX line.
6. Twist on the Ninja blade and blend until smooth.

CHEF'S NOTE

This is a really lovely fruity nut smoothie. Add a few blueberries too if you like.

SERVES 1

DOUBLE ALMOND SWEET POTATO SMOOTHIE

270 calories

Ingredients

VITAMIN B+

- 50g/2oz spinach
- 150g/5oz sweet potato
- 200ml/7floz unsweetened almond milk
- 1 tbsp ground almonds
- Water

Method

1 Rinse the ingredients well.

2 Remove any thick stalks from the spinach.

3 Cube the sweet potato, no need to peel.

4 Add the spinach, sweet potato, almond milk & ground almonds to the Ninja large (24oz) cup. Make sure the ingredients do not go past the MAX line on your machine.

5 Add a little water if needed to take it up to the MAX line.

6 Twist on the Ninja blade and blend until smooth.

CHEF'S NOTE

Sweet potatoes are an exceptionally rich source of vitamin A.

SERVES 1

VITAMIN C JUICE BOOST

240 calories

Ingredients

NUTRIENT DENSE

- 150g/5oz kiwis
- 150g/5oz oranges
- 150g/5oz apple
- Water

Method

1. Rinse the ingredients well.
2. Peel the kiwi. Peel and de-seed the orange.
3. Core the apple.
4. Add the fruit to the Ninja large (24oz) cup. Make sure the ingredients do not go past the MAX line on your machine.
5. Add water, again being careful not to exceed the MAX line.
6. Twist on the Ninja blade and blend until smooth.

CHEF'S NOTE

With its fruit combo this juice delivers triple Vitamin C goodness.

SERVES 1

TROPICAL FRUIT PICKUP

260 calories

Ingredients

VITAMIN C COMBO

- 150g/5oz mango
- 150g/5oz pineapple
- 1 small banana
- Water

Method

1. Rinse the ingredients well.
2. Peel the pineapple and banana.
3. Peel & de-stone the mango.
4. Add the fruit to the Ninja large (24oz) cup. Make sure the ingredients do not go past the MAX line on your machine.
5. Add water, again being careful not to exceed the MAX line.
6. Twist on the Ninja blade and blend until smooth.

CHEF'S NOTE

You could try making with soya milk too (but this will increase calories).

SERVES 1

BEETROOT & SOYA MILK SMOOTHIE

297 calories

Ingredients

- 150g/5oz beetroot
- 150g/5oz orange
- 1 small banana
- 200ml/7floz soya milk
- Water

Method

1. Rinse the ingredients well.
2. Peel the beetroot, orange & banana.
3. Add the beetroot, fruit & soya milk to the Ninja large (24oz) cup. Make sure the ingredients do not go past the MAX line on your machine.
4. Add a little water if needed to take it up to the MAX line.
5. Twist on the Ninja blade and blend until smooth.

CHEF'S NOTE

The beetroot gives this smoothie a lovely ruby glow.

SERVES 1

KALE & HONEY JUICE

240 calories

Ingredients

NUTRITIOUS

- 75g/3oz kale
- 150g/5oz pineapple
- 150g/5oz apple
- 2 tsp honey
- Water

Method

1 Rinse the ingredients well.

2 Cut any thick stalks off the kale.

3 Peel the pineapple. Core the apple.

4 Add the kale, fruit & honey to the Ninja large (24oz) cup. Make sure the ingredients do not go past the MAX line on your machine.

5 Add water, again being careful not to exceed the MAX line.

6 Twist on the Ninja blade and blend until smooth.

CHEF'S NOTE

Low in calories, high in fibre and with zero fat, kale is a mega smoothie super-food.

SERVES 1

MANGO & FLAX SEED SMOOTHIE

246 calories

Ingredients

- 75g/3oz spinach
- 150g/5oz mango
- 1 small banana
- 2 tbsp flax seeds
- Water

Method

1. Rinse the ingredients well.
2. Cut any thick stalks off the spinach.
3. Peel and stone the mango.
4. Peel the banana.
5. Add the spinach, mango, banana & flax seeds to the Ninja large (24oz) cup. Make sure the ingredients do not go past the MAX line on your machine.
6. Add water, again being careful not to exceed the MAX line.
7. Twist on the Ninja blade and blend until smooth.

CHEF'S NOTE

Flax seeds add a boost of protein and fibre to your smoothie blend.

SERVES 1

RASPBERRY GRAPE JUICE

257 calories

Ingredients

NATURALLY SWEET

- 150g/5oz raspberries
- 150g/5oz seedless green grapes
- 150g/5oz apple
- Water

Method

1 Rinse the ingredients well.

2 Core the apple.

3 Add the fruit to the Ninja large (24oz) cup. Make sure the ingredients do not go past the MAX line or your machine.

4 Add water, again being careful not to exceed the MAX line.

5 Twist on the Ninja blade and blend until smooth.

CHEF'S NOTE

A handful of spinach or kale adds a little green goodness to this sweet fruit juice.

TRIPLE GREEN GOODNESS

SERVES 1

205 calories

Ingredients

- 50g/2oz spinach
- 50g/2oz kale
- 125g/4oz asparagus
- 1 small banana
- 1 tbsp chia seeds
- Water

Method

1 Rinse the ingredients well.

2 Cut any thick stalks off the kale and spinach

3 Peel the banana.

4 Add the vegetables, fruit & chia seeds to the Ninja large (24oz) cup. Make sure the ingredients do not go past the MAX line on your machine.

5 Add water, again being careful not to exceed the MAX line.

6 Twist on the Ninja blade and blend until smooth.

CHEF'S NOTE

Use only the sweet tips of the asparagus. Discard the thick woody ends

SERVES 1

AVOCADO & APPLE JUICE

297 calories

Ingredients

SMOOTH & RICH

- 50g/2oz spinach
- 75g/3oz avocado
- 100g/3½oz apple
- 1 small banana
- Water

Method

1 Rinse the ingredients well.

2 Cut any thick stalks off the spinach

3 Peel & stone the avocado. Core the apple & peel the banana.

4 Add the vegetables & fruit to the Ninja large (24oz) cup. Make sure the ingredients do not go past the MAX line on your machine.

5 Add water, again being careful not to exceed the MAX line.

6 Twist on the Ninja blade and blend until smooth.

CHEF'S NOTE

Avocado is a nutrient dense food that also adds luxurious smoothness to smoothies.

SERVES 1

SOYA MILK SUNSHINE

250 calories

Ingredients

- 150g/5oz apple
- 150g/5oz orange
- 200ml/7floz soya milk
- 1 tsp honey
- Water

Method

1. Rinse the ingredients well.
2. Peel and de-seed the orange.
3. Core the apple.
4. Add the fruit, honey & soya milk to the Ninja large (24oz) cup. Make sure the ingredients do not go past the MAX line on your machine.
5. Add a little water if needed to take it up to the MAX line.
6. Twist on the Ninja blade and blend until smooth.

CHEF'S NOTE

Almond milk works just as well for this fresh & bright smoothie.

SERVES 1

CREAMY CASHEW SMOOTHIE

280 calories

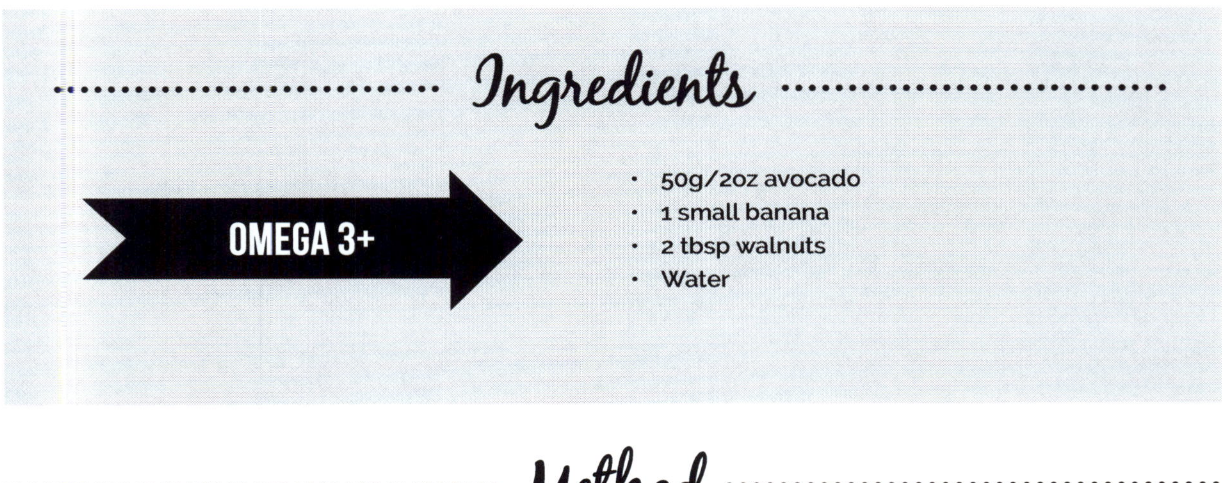

Ingredients

- 50g/2oz avocado
- 1 small banana
- 2 tbsp walnuts
- Water

Method

1. Rinse the ingredients well.
2. Peel & stone the avocado. Peel the banana.
3. Add the avocado, banana & walnuts to the Ninja large (24oz) cup. Make sure the ingredients do not go past the MAX line on your machine.
4. Add water, again being careful not to exceed the MAX line.
5. Twist on the Ninja blade and blend until smooth.

CHEF'S NOTE

Walnuts contain anti-inflammatory properties.

CHIA MILK SMOOTHIE

SERVES 1

270
calories

Ingredients

PROTEIN+

- 50g/2oz spinach
- 300ml/10½floz soya milk
- 2 tbsp chia seeds
- Water

Method

1 Rinse the spinach and remove any thick stalks.

2 Add the spinach, soya milk & chia seeds to the Ninja large (24oz) cup. Make sure the ingredients do not go past the MAX line on your machine.

3 Add a little water if needed to take it up to the MAX line.

4 Twist on the Ninja blade and blend until smooth.

CHEF'S NOTE

Chia seeds are thought to aid weight loss by helping to control hunger.

SUPER SEEDS SMOOTHIE

SERVES 1

277 calories

Ingredients

NUTRIENT RICH

- 75g/3oz spinach
- 300ml/10½floz almond milk
- 1 tbsp chia seeds
- 1 tbsp flax seeds
- Water

Method

1 Rinse the spinach and remove any thick stalks.

2 Add the spinach, almond milk & seeds to the Ninja large (24oz) cup. Make sure the ingredients do not go past the MAX line on your machine.

3 Add a little water if needed to take it up to the MAX line.

4 Twist on the Ninja blade and blend until smooth.

CHEF'S NOTE

This double blast of healthy seeds is packed with essential omega-3's.

SERVES 1

PINEAPPLE & GINGER SMOOTHIE

291 calories

Ingredients

- 50g/2oz spinach
- 200g/7oz pineapple
- 1 small banana
- 200ml/7floz almond milk
- 2cm/1 inch peeled fresh ginger root
- Water

Method

1. Rinse the ingredients well.
2. Remove any thick stalks from the spinach.
3. Peel the pineapple & banana.
4. Add the spinach, fruit, almond milk & ginger to the Ninja large (24oz) cup. Make sure the ingredients do not go past the MAX line on your machine.
5. Add a little water if needed to take it up to the MAX line.
6. Twist on the Ninja blade and blend until smooth.

CHEF'S NOTE

Ginger has a long tradition of being used to aid the digestive system.

SERVES 1

CARROT & ALMOND MILK SMOOTHIE

267 calories

Ingredients

DOUBLE NUT

- 200g/7oz carrots
- 150g/5oz strawberries
- 200ml/7floz almond milk
- 1 tbsp ground almonds
- Water

Method

1. Rinse the ingredients well.
2. Top & tail the carrots, no need to peel.
3. Add the carrots, strawberries almond milk & ground almonds to the Ninja large (24oz) cup. Make sure the ingredients do not go past the MAX line on your machine.
4. Add a little water if needed to take it up to the MAX line.
5. Twist on the Ninja blade and blend until smooth.

CHEF'S NOTE

High protein almonds are rich in Vitamin E and are ideal for sating the appetite.

SERVES 1

GOJI BERRY & BANANA SMOOTHIE

226 calories

Ingredients

- 50g/2oz spinach
- 1 small banana
- 300ml/10½ floz unsweetened almond milk
- 3 tbsp goji berries
- Water

Method

1 Rinse the ingredients well.

2 Remove any thick stalks from the spinach.

3 Peel the banana.

4 Add the spinach, banana, almond milk & goji berries to the Ninja large (24oz) cup. Make sure the ingredients do not go past the MAX line on your machine.

5 Add a little water if needed to take it up to the MAX line.

6 Twist on the Ninja blade and blend until smooth.

CHEF'S NOTE

High in antioxidants Goji berries contain vitamin C, vitamin B2, vitamin A, iron & selenium.

SERVES 1

SPRING GREEN FRUIT JUICE

230 calories

Ingredients

QUICK & EASY!

- 50g/2oz shredded spring greens
- 250g/9oz apple
- 1 small banana
- Water

Method

1 Rinse the ingredients well.

2 Core the apple and peel the banana.

3 Add the spring greens & fruit to the Ninja large (24oz) cup. Make sure the ingredients do not go past the MAX line on your machine.

4 Add water, again being careful not to exceed the MAX line.

5 Twist on the Ninja blade and blend until smooth.

CHEF'S NOTE

Bags of pre-prepared shredded greens are really useful to pick up as a quick smoothie ingredient.

SERVES 1

SWEET POTATO & COCONUT MILK SMOOTHIE

296 calories

Ingredients

VITAMIN A +

- 50g/2oz spinach
- 150g/5oz sweet potato
- 200ml/7floz light coconut milk
- Water

Method

1. Rinse the ingredients well.
2. Remove any thick stalks from the spinach.
3. Cube the sweet potato, no need to peel.
4. Add the spinach, sweet potato & coconut milk to the Ninja large (24oz) cup. Make sure the ingredients do not go past the MAX line on your machine.
5. Add a little water if needed to take it up to the MAX line.
6. Twist on the Ninja blade and blend until smooth.

CHEF'S NOTE

Use low fat coconut milk, you'll loose a bit of the creaminess but the calories are much lower than the full fat version.

SERVES 1

SWEET TENDERSTEM BROCCOLI JUICE

230 calories

Ingredients

ENERGY BOOST

- 125g/4oz tenderstem broccoli/broccolini
- 125g/4oz apple
- 125g/4oz carrot
- 1 tbsp chia seeds
- Water

Method

1 Rinse the ingredients well.

2 Core the apple and top & tail the carrot.

3 Add the broccoli, carrot, apple & chia seeds to the Ninja large (24oz) cup. Make sure the ingredients do not go past the MAX line on your machine.

4 Add water, again being careful not to exceed the MAX line.

5 Twist on the Ninja blade and blend until smooth.

CHEF'S NOTE

Tenderstem broccoli has a more delicate flavour than its full-bodied relatives.

SERVES 1

HONEY & APPLE JUICE

232 calories

Ingredients

- 50g/2oz spinach
- 200g/7oz apple
- 1 small banana
- 2 tsp honey
- Water

Method

1 Rinse the ingredients well.

2 Remove any thick stalks from the spinach.

3 Core the apple and peel the banana.

4 Add the spinach, fruit & honey to the Ninja large (24oz) cup. Make sure the ingredients do not go past the MAX line on your machine.

5 Add water, again being careful not to exceed the MAX line.

6 Twist on the Ninja blade and blend until smooth.

CHEF'S NOTE

Always use a sweet tasting apple rather than a sharp cooking apple for smoothies and juices.

SERVES 1

BANANA & CHIA SEED SMOOTHIE

245 calories

Ingredients

OMEGA 3+

- 50g/2oz spinach
- 2 small bananas
- 1 tbsp chia seeds
- Water

Method

1 Rinse the spinach well.

2 Remove any thick stalks from the spinach.

3 Peel the bananas.

4 Add the spinach, bananas & chia seeds to the Ninja large (24oz) cup. Make sure the ingredients do not go past the MAX line on your machine.

5 Add water, again being careful not to exceed the MAX line.

6 Twist on the Ninja blade and blend until smooth.

CHEF'S NOTE

Soya milk also works well in this protein rich banana smoothie

SERVES 1

CHERRY & ALMOND MILK SMOOTHIE

295 calories

Ingredients

- 50g/2oz spinach
- 100g/3½oz pitted cherries
- 1 small banana
- 200ml/11floz unsweetened almond milk
- Water

Method

1 Rinse the ingredients well.

2 Remove any thick stalks from the spinach.

3 Peel the banana. Make sure you have removed all the stalks and stones from the cherries.

4 Add the spinach, fruit & almond milk to the Ninja large (24oz) cup. Make sure the ingredients do not go past the MAX line on your machine.

5 Add a little water if needed to take it up to the MAX line.

6 Twist on the Ninja blade and blend until smooth.

CHEF'S NOTE

Cherries are rich in queritrin which has been found by researchers to be one of the most potent anti-cancer agents.

SERVES 1

TURMERIC GREEN JUICE

220 calories

Ingredients

DIGESTION AID

- 50g/2oz spinach
- 50g/2oz kale
- 200g/7oz apple
- ½-1 tsp ground turmeric
- 1 tbsp chia seeds
- Water

Method

1 Rinse the ingredients well.

2 Remove any thick stalks from the spinach and kale.

3 Core the apple.

4 Nip the ends of the cucumber, don't bother peeling.

5 Add the fruit, vegetables & turmeric to the Ninja large (24oz) cup. Make sure the ingredients do not go past the MAX line on your machine.

6 Add water, again being careful not to exceed the MAX line.

7 Twist on the Ninja blade and blend until smooth.

CHEF'S NOTE

Turmeric is a natural anti-inflammatory which has been used in Chinese medicine throughout the ages.

SERVES 1

PROTEIN CRANBERRY SMOOTHIE

297 calories

Ingredients

- 150g/5oz cranberries
- 1 small banana
- 200ml/7floz unsweetened almond milk
- 1 tbsp flax seeds
- Water

Method

1 Rinse the ingredients well.

2 Peel the banana.

3 Add the fruit, flax seeds & almond milk to the Ninja large (24oz) cup. Make sure the ingredients do not go past the MAX line on your machine.

4 Add a little water if needed to take it up to the MAX line.

5 Twist on the Ninja blade and blend until smooth.

CHEF'S NOTE

High in protein and fibre, flax seeds are also thought to have a positive effect in helping to lower blood pressure.

SERVES 1

LIME & APPLE JUICE

222
calories

Ingredients

DETOX JUICE

- 50g/2oz spinach
- 400g/7oz apples
- 3 tbsp lime juice
- Water

Method

1 Rinse the ingredients well.

2 Remove any thick stalks from the spinach.

3 Core the apples.

4 Add the spinach, apples & lime juice to the Ninja large (24oz) cup. Make sure the ingredients do not go past the MAX line on your machine.

5 Add water, again being careful not to exceed the MAX line.

6 Twist on the Ninja blade and blend until smooth.

CHEF'S NOTE

Adjust the lime to suit your own taste in this zingy juice.

SERVES 1

AVOCADO & SPINACH SMOOTHIE

299 calories

Ingredients

- 50g/2oz spinach
- 75g/3oz avocado
- 75g/3oz apple
- 200ml/7floz unsweetened almond milk
- Water

Method

1. Rinse the ingredients well.
2. Remove any thick stalks from the spinach.
3. Peel & stone the avocado. Core the apple.
4. Add the fruit, vegetables & almond milk to the Ninja large (24oz) cup. Make sure the ingredients do not go past the MAX line on your machine.
5. Add a little water if needed to take it up to the MAX line.
6. Twist on the Ninja blade and blend until smooth.

CHEF'S NOTE

Avocado and spinach make a lovely vitamin rich smoothie combination.

SERVES 1

BANANA & COCONUT WATER SMOOTHIE

250 calories

Ingredients

HEALTH BOOSTER

- 50g/2oz spinach
- 2 small bananas
- 300ml/11floz coconut water
- 1 tbsp pumpkin seeds
- Water

Method

1 Rinse the ingredients well.

2 Cut any thick green stalks off the spinach.

3 Peel the bananas.

4 Add the spinach, bananas, coconut water & pumpkin seeds to the Ninja large (24oz) cup. Make sure the ingredients do not go past the MAX line on your machine.

5 Add a little water if needed to take it up to the MAX line.

6 Twist on the Ninja blade and blend until smooth.

CHEF'S NOTE

Use only one banana if you prefer a lighter consistency.

GREEN CASHEW MILK

SERVES 1

289 calories

Ingredients

- 50g/2oz spinach
- 175g/6oz apple
- 200ml/7floz unsweetened almond milk
- 2 tbsp cashews
- Water

Method

1 Rinse the ingredients well.

2 Remove any thick stalks from the spinach.

3 Core the apple.

4 Add the fruit, vegetables, cashews & almond milk to the Ninja large (24oz) cup. Make sure the ingredients do not go past the MAX line on your machine.

5 Add a little water if needed to take it up to the MAX line.

6 Twist on the Ninja blade and blend until smooth.

CHEF'S NOTE

Cashew nuts may be low in fibre but they are packed with vitamins, minerals & antioxidants.

SERVES 1

APPLE & DATE SOYA SMOOTHIE

295 calories

Ingredients

SWEET & NUTRITIOUS

- 150g/5oz apple
- 50g/2oz pitted dates
- 200ml/7floz soya milk
- Water

Method

1 Rinse the ingredients well.

2 Core the apple.

3 Add the fruit & soya milk to the Ninja large (24oz) cup. Make sure the ingredients do not go past the MAX line on your machine.

4 Add a little water if needed to take it up to the MAX line.

5 Twist on the Ninja blade and blend until smooth.

CHEF'S NOTE

Use dried unsweetened dates and ensure all the stones are removed.

SERVES 1

STRAWBERRY & PUMPKIN SEED SMOOTHIE

238 calories

Ingredients

- 150g/5oz strawberries
- 1 small banana
- 200ml/7floz soya milk
- 1 tbsp pumpkin seeds
- Water

Method

1 Rinse the ingredients well.

2 Remove any green tops from the strawberries.

3 Peel the banana.

4 Add the fruit, soya milk & pumpkin seeds to the Ninja large (24oz) cup. Make sure the ingredients do not go past the MAX line on your machine.

5 Add a little water if needed to take it up to the MAX line.

6 Twist on the Ninja blade and blend until smooth.

CHEF'S NOTE

For an additional protein blast add a teaspoon of flax seeds.

Other COOKNATION TITLES

If you enjoyed 'The *Skinny* NUTRI NINJA Recipe Book' you may also be interested in the *Skinny* NUTRiBULLET titles in the CookNation series.

Visit **www.bellmackenzie.com** to browse the full catalogue.

THE Skinny
NUTRiBULLET
RECIPE BOOK
CookNation

THE Skinny
NUTRiBULLET
7 DAY CLEANSE
CookNation

THE Skinny
NUTRiBULLET
MEALS IN MINUTES
RECIPE BOOK
CookNation

THE Skinny
NUTRiBULLET
SOUP
RECIPE BOOK
CookNation

THE Skinny
NUTRiBULLET
SUPER GREEN SMOOTHIES
CookNation

THE Skinny
NUTRiBULLET
SLIMMING SMOOTHIES
CookNation

THE Skinny
NUTRiBULLET
5:2 DIET
SMOOTHIES
CookNation

THE
NUTRiBULLET
Cocktail
Book
CookNation